D1411880

The Vietnam Veterans Memorial

Ted and Lola Schaefer

Heinemann Library
Chicago, Illinois

© 2006 Heinemann Library
a division of Reed Elsevier Inc.
Chicago, Illinois

Customer Service 888-454-2279

Visit our website at www.heinemannlibrary.com

Designed by Richard Parker and Mike Hogg Design
Illustrations by Jeff Edwards
Originated by Chroma Graphics (Overseas) Pte. Ltd
Printed and bound in China by South China Printing Company

10 09 08 07 06
10 9 8 7 6 5 4 3 2 1

Library of Congress Cataloging-in-Publication Data
Schaefer, Ted, 1948-
  The Vietnam Veterans Memorial / Ted and Lola M. Schaefer.
     p. cm. -- (Symbols of freedom)
  Includes index.
  ISBN 1-4034-6659-9 (lib. bdg.) -- ISBN 1-4034-6668-8 (pbk.)
  1. Vietnam Veterans Memorial (Washington, D.C.)--Juvenile literature. I. Schaefer, Lola M., 1950- II. Title. III. Series.
  DS559.83.W18.S36 2005
  959.704'36--dc22
                               2005002041

J
917.53
SCH
c. 1

Acknowledgments
The publishers would like to thank the following for permission to reproduce photographs:
Corbis p. 24, pp. 12, 14, 16 (Bettman), 15 (Bettman/Mal Langsden), 18 (James P. Blair), 21, 27 (Richard Hamilton Smith), 17 (Wally McNamee); Getty Images pp. 6, 9, 10, 11, 13 (Hulton Archive); Jill Birschbach/Harcourt Education Ltd pp. 4, 5, 19, 20, 22, 23, 25, 28, 29; Topham Picturepoint p. 7.

Cover photograph of the Vietnam Veterans Memorial reproduced with permission of Jill Birschbach/Harcourt Education Ltd.

The publishers would like to thank Duery Felton Jr., Curator of the Vietnam Veterans Memorial Collection, for his assistance in the preparation of this book.

In recognition of the National Park Service Rangers who are always present at the memorials, offering general information and interpretative tours. We thank you!

Every effort has been made to contact copyright holders of any material reproduced in this book. Any omissions will be rectified in subsequent printings if notice is given to the publishers.

The publishers and authors have done their best to ensure the accuracy and currency of all the information in this book, however, they can accept no responsibility for any loss, injury, or inconvenience sustained as a result of information or advice contained in the book.

Some words are shown in bold, **like this**. You can find out what they mean by looking in the glossary.

Contents

The Vietnam Veterans Memorial

The Vietnam Veterans **Memorial** is in
Washington, D.C., near the Potomac River.
The land around the memorial is grassy and
open like a park.

4

The memorial is a place for people to remember the **servicemen** and **servicewomen** who died in the **Vietnam War**. It also remembers those who are still missing.

The Fighting Men and Women

More than 2.5 million American men and women served in the **Vietnam War**. They came from all kinds of families and from every state.

These soldiers were very young. Many were only nineteen years old. Most men chose to join the U.S. **military forces**, but some were **drafted**.

The Vietnam War

Vietnam was a divided country. North Vietnam had a **communist** government that ruled by force. Their armies tried to take over South Vietnam.

Other communist countries helped North Vietnam. The people of South Vietnam could not fight alone. The United States sent soldiers and money to help them.

Years of Fighting

At first the American people wanted the U.S. soldiers to be in Vietnam. They knew South Vietnam needed help. But the war was long and very hard.

People in the United States watched the
Vietnam War on television every night. They
saw pain and death. Many people wanted the
war to end.

Veterans Come Home

The United States won all of their **battles**, but they did not win the war. In 1973 the U.S. government brought their soldiers home from Vietnam.

Not everyone welcomed home the soldiers. There were no big celebrations or parades. People just wanted to forget about the war.

Time for a Memorial

Jan Scruggs was a Vietnam **veteran**. He remembered his friends and the others who died in the **Vietnam War**. He wanted a **memorial** for them.

1975

Jan Scruggs found other people who wanted
a Vietnam memorial. They raised money and
looked for **designs**. The U.S. government
gave them land in Washington, D.C.

Building a Memorial

Maya Ying Lin sent a **design** that they liked. She planned a **memorial** that would look like part of the land.

In the spring of 1982, workers began building the memorial. Eight months later, it was finished. **Veterans** from around the country came for the five-day **dedication**.

The Wall

Two **granite** walls form the Vietnam Veterans **Memorial**. Each rises from the ground at one end until they meet at the highest point in the middle.

Each wall is made of polished granite.
It **reflects** light like a mirror. Visitors can
see themselves as they look at the memorial.

The Names

More than 58,000 U.S. soldiers died in Vietnam or are still missing. The name of each one is cut into the walls of the **memorial**.

EGINALD W...
ENNETH J FARRELL · GEORGE F FLANAGAN
L · BILLY W GOBER · ROGER D GRIFFITH ·
LARRY H McLAUGHLIN · BILLY GENE JENT ·
ROGER W LARCHER · RICHARD L LONG ·
ONTAGUE · THOMAS McCRAY · BOBBY F HOLMA
GENE A POLITO · GARRY G PRINCE ·
VID L SIMON · DAVID R SIMONS ·
RANK OLIVARES TABOADA · KENNETH J TAKEMOTO
OBERT V VINSCOTSKI · RONALD R WATSON ·
NMAN · ERNEST F BRIGGS Jr · LARRY I BRIGGS
ARTHUR J EARLES · SIDNEY H COOLER ·
S · RICHARD E DEVORE · LARRY A DIEFENBACH
NTI · SAMUEL FANTLE III · RALPH E FOULKS
HJOHNSON · JAMES

A **diamond** next to a name shows that soldier was killed in the war. A cross next to a name shows that man is still missing.

The Three Servicemen

This **bronze sculpture** of "The Three Servicemen" is part of the **memorial**. It stands on a small hill. The three men seem to be looking toward the walls.

There is an American flag nearby and
another bronze sculpture. This sculpture
remembers the women who served in the
armed forces during the **Vietnam War**.

Saying Thank You and Goodbye

People visit the Vietnam Veterans **Memorial** every day and night. Some bring medals, flags, or army boots. They leave these near the names of people they knew.

Others bring personal **mementos**, such as photos, letters, or toys. This is one way that families and friends say thank you or goodbye.

Visiting the Vietnam Veterans Memorial

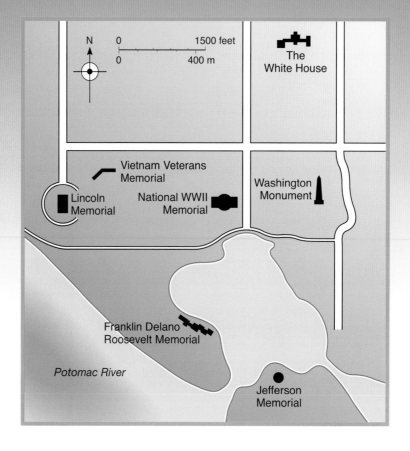

Here is a map of the **National Mall** showing the Vietnam Veterans **Memorial**. One wall points to the Lincoln Memorial. The other wall points to the Washington Monument.

When you visit the Vietnam Veterans Memorial, look at all the names. Think about these soldiers who gave their lives fighting for **freedom**.

Fact File

Vietnam Veterans Memorial

★ The Vietnam Veterans **Memorial** Fund received 1,421 **designs**. They laid them out in an airplane hangar and carefully looked at each one.

★ The Vietnam Veterans Memorial cost approximately $9 million. Many different people gave this money.

★ Around 25 **mementos** are left at the memorial each day. Park rangers collect them and keep them in the Museum Resource Center. More than 75,000 mementos have been saved since the opening of the Vietnam Veterans Memorial.

★ The largest memento left at the Wall was a motorcycle. The Rolling Thunder Group brought it on **Memorial Day**.

Timeline

Vietnam Veterans Memorial

★ 1954   Vietnam divides into North Vietnam and South Vietnam

★ 1965   President Johnson sends U.S. **troops** to South Vietnam

★ 1973   United States and North Vietnam sign Paris agreements, ending American fighting in the war

★ 1979   Jan Scruggs gets idea for a **memorial** to remember those who served in Vietnam

★ 1980   President Jimmy Carter signs a bill saving land in Washington, D.C. for the memorial

★ 1981   Maya Ying Lin's **design** is chosen for the Vietnam Veterans Memorial

★ 1982   Building of the memorial begins in March; the Vietnam Veterans Memorial is finished and **dedicated** in November

Glossary

battle fight between two armies

bronze hard, reddish brown metal that is a mixture of copper and tin

communist form of government that believes everything is owned by the government and shared equally by all the people

dedicate have a ceremony that opens a new bridge, hospital, or memorial

design draw the shape and style of something

diamond shape with four equal sides, like a square standing on one of its corners

draft when the government chooses people to serve as soldiers

freedom having the right to say, behave, or move around as you please

granite hard rock often used as a building material

memento object that is a reminder of a place or person

memorial something that is built to help people remember a person or an event

Memorial Day holiday celebrated in the United States on the last Monday of May to honor Americans who have died in wars

military forces all the branches of a country's military; in the United States the military forces include the Army, Navy, Air Force, Marine Corps, and Coast Guard

National Mall large, park-like area of land in Washington, D.C. where museums and memorials are built

reflect show an image of something on a shiny surface

sculpture something carved or shaped out of stone, wood, metal, marble, or clay

servicemen/servicewomen people who are soldiers in the military forces

veteran someone who has served in the armed forces

Vietnam War war fought on the ground of South Vietnam. The U.S. armed forces fought with the South Vietnam military against the armies of North Vietnam.

More Books to Read

An older reader can help you with these books:

Britton, Tamara L. *The Vietnam Veterans Memorial.* Edina, Minn.: ABDO, 2004.

DeCapua, Sarah. *The Vietnam Veterans Memorial.* N.Y.: Children's Press, 2003.

Dubois, Muriel L. *The Vietnam Veterans Memorial.* Mankato, Minn.: Bridgestone Books, 2002.

Ferry, Joseph. *The Vietnam Veterans Memorial.* Philadelphia, Pa.: Mason Crest, 2003.

Visiting the Memorial

The Vietnam Veterans Memorial is open every day of the year, except Christmas Day (December 25), 8:30 A.M. to midnight. Park rangers are present during these times to answer questions or give talks on the memorial.

To ask for a brochure and map of the Vietnam Veterans Memorial, write to this address:

National Park Service
900 Ohio Drive SW
Washington, D.C. 20024.

Index